Basic Biblical Teaching Skills

*+Marshall Gilmore
Bishop 4-8-94
Classmate in
epimopary of*

Bishop Dotcy Ivertus Isom, Jr.

Published By The
Christian Methodist Episcopal Church
General Board of Publication Services
Memphis, Tennessee

84910

TABLE OF CONTENTS

ACKNOWLEDGMENTS

Without the grace and guidance of God, the completion of this project would have been utterly impossible. In thanking God for this project, I am also aware that there were several other helping agents. Of course, I want to thank my wife, Mrs. Ester L. Isom for her unselfish attitude in loaning me her ears, as well as her thoughts. A word of thanks to my Administrative Assistant, Mrs. Cora M. Williams, and Rev. Clarence C. Buchannan, Program Director for the Third Episcopal District. Thank you for helping me implement what I have written.

It has truly been a challenge for me to develop a literary piece such as this, while at the same time tend to the pertinent matters of the Episcopacy. Nevertheless, God blessed me with the vision of what is contained between the covers of this book, and a dedicated editorial staff. Thanks to Rev. Juan M. Turnes for sharing his ideas, and a special word of thanks to the editors of this book, Dr. Geoffrey D. Nealy and Rev. George W. Coleman. Jr.

To God be the glory and the praise for whatever spiritual insight is obtained by those who share in this book.

INTRODUCTION

In this vast world of ours we have been equipped with the abilities of learning and teaching. Fortunately, learning can be accomplished even at an involuntary mode. As we go through life, there are things we learn even when we are not trying to learn. When we hear our children explain their feelings to us, we learn the true meaning of sincerity. When we see our parents ripen in age, we learn that our life is only a brief paragraph in the pages of history.

Learning is innate! All of creation is endowed with the ability to learn. At the early stage of birth the baby opossum learns to cling to the back of its mother. Upon entering the world, the newborn child immediately learns that in order to survive he/she must inhale and exhale air. The child does not understand the anatomical functions, but the child has learned that breathing is necessary. Learning is part of all of our lives, and more than often, it is a process that presents itself to us, even when weeds not see it.

But what about teaching? This process is not conquered so easily. Teaching is a process that requires an initiative on the teacher's behalf. In other words, an effort has to be made on behalf of the teacher to develop a channel of communication, which will adequately convey a message to the observer. Sure! There are some things we involuntarily teach. Nevertheless, we know that meaningful learning experiences derive from committed teaching and well developed teaching skills. Some of the greatest teaching most of us received were the lessons of life, conveyed to us by our parents/guardians. But we should not take for granted the commitment they had for passing on to us the revelations they had received in their journey through life. They used their tools of common sense and hind sight to share with us some of life's best kept secrets. Their teaching skills were not developed out of any academic curriculum, but they made sure we got the message. They did all they could to make sure that the concepts of life that they had pieced together touched our ears, mind, and hearts. Their commitment to help us avoid the pitfalls of life is the same type of self commitment that is needed to effectively teach any subject and in any setting.

Chapter 1
Teaching from a Biblical Perspective

In looking at teaching from a biblical perspective, the same commitment and pursuance our ancestors had, are called upon in understanding, interpreting, and sharing God's Holy Word. No one is born with all the knowledge of God's word. Our understanding of Scripture begins with the simplest form of teaching. We read and our traditionally set minds interpret. What we have seen and what we have been taught by society and the human beings that surround us, lend a helping hand in our development of what we read. While this is inescapable, it alone is not enough! When we leave our understanding of God's word in the hands of traditionalism, we risk seeing and hearing God's word from a one-sided, and often times, a distorted view of things. Our understanding of God's word encompasses the task of getting as close as possible to what Rudolph Bultmann calls "original meaning" (Bultmann, *The Problem of Hermeneutics*, page113) and understanding ancient history in modern times. To hear Scripture is not enough. To read it in the realms of only our own close-circuit lives is nothing less than meagerly robbing the rich treasure houses of wisdom. If the betterment of our society depends on our understanding and sharing God's word, then we must take seriously the concept of teaching. If we become comfortable with the idea of the rich resources of our minds dwelling in a cozy nest of complacency, the components of teaching will go untapped.

Enlightenment always awaits those who seek the understanding of God's words and commit themselves to sharing it with others.

TEACHING FROM AN OLD TESTAMENT PERSPECTIVE

In Deuteronomy 6:7, God instructs the people of Israel to teach their children diligently His commandments:

> And you shall teach them diligently to your children, and shall talk of them when you sit in your house, and when you walk by the way, and when you lie down, and when you rise (RSV).

It was not enough that one generation had developed a relationship with God. It was not enough that the younger generation had learned bits and pieces about their history and where they came from. From reading the 6th chapter of Deuteronomy it is quite evident that God wanted what one generation had learned, passed on to other generations. Even more, the teaching of God's commandments were to be taught in every facet of life. When God told the children of Israel to digest the word of God into every entity of life (vv.6-9), the underlying message was, that the teaching of God's commandments was to be a part of everyday life. Although the concept of teaching can be found throughout the Old Testament, the passages of Scripture listed earlier (Deut. 6:6-9) clearly validates the point that religious teaching was a way of life. In all of God's omnipotence God knew that in order for humankind to practice a way of life that would draw them closer to salvation, there would need to be a commitment to teaching; not teaching that took place one day a week, for approximately two to three hours. But rather, committed teaching that used every available resource and opportunity to help reveal God's message to humanity.

God recognized a need for humanity to have spiritual roots. By now, most of humanity has realized that a spiritually rootless generation cannot survive. Even with all the amenities of this twentieth century, we still feel that our livelihood lies in jeopardy. Too many times we have seen those who practically had it all, take their life. We have seen beautifully sculptured mansions destroyed by the iniquitous forces of nature. In any and all the arenas of life, we are reminded that we live in a temporal world. And the reality of finitude ignites in our minds, the need for a God of infinity. Now, why say all of this? All of this was said so that together, we see that as open minded, somewhat intelligent beings, we recognize the need of a powerful and loving God, and at the same time recognize that there is a need to learn of our God. How is this done? This can only be accomplished through following the same instructions God gave the children of Israel: "And these words, which I command thee this day, shall be in thine heart: And thou shalt teach them diligently unto thy children..."(vv.6-7a). The spiritual power that undergirded the early Hebrews' life, was the same spiritual power God wanted the people to teach to their children. How else would the power of God be understood? How could a faithless generation possibly come to the realization of God's commandments? There had to be a commitment to teaching. Although we have come a long ways since the writing of the Old Testament, the need for a close relationship with God still exists. Most of all, there still remains the need for committed teachers, who can truly assist in teaching humans what it is to live in a personal relationship with God. The impact of the Old Testament on teaching should result in making its words and themes increasingly accessible to the needs of people living today. If this does not happen, something is amiss in our preaching, teaching, and understanding of God's words, and it must be corrected.

When we approach the Old Testament from a teaching perspective, we must keep in mind the genuine goals of the Old Testament writers. For the most part, the writers developed, borrowed, and recorded through revelations various accounts and stories for the purpose of teaching the great truths that God had laid upon their hearts. With the Old Testament, the most important point to be recognized, however, is that the biblical writers received their stories in their tradition and used these in their witness. Having received their revelation from God, they used the ancient stories as instruments to express, convey, and teach the truth that God had placed upon their hearts. The Old Testament, especially the Pentateuch (first five books of the Bible), is more than a glimpse of ancient Hebrew living. The Old Testament is an icon of the teaching/learning process the people went through as they travelled through life.

RELAYING THE BATH QOL OF THE OLD TESTAMENT

The term Bath Qol (also Bat Kol) is the name given to a heavenly voice which revealed God's will to humankind (Soulen, *Handbook of Biblical Criticism*, page 28). In essence, the Bath Qol is God's direct communication with humans. The concept of teaching in the Old Testament centers around communicating/teaching the will of God, but it is the word of God which is received by a human so that it can be taught to other humans. That was how teaching was seen during the early biblical days. The parents committed themselves to teaching their children the will of God because they had heard the Bath Qol and it instructed them to teach God's commandments to the people. It was God who called the children of Israel to the task of teaching

4

God's ways to the entire Jewish community.

Out of all the reasons to teach, what better reason than to teach because we have heard the Bath Qol from on high, telling us to convey to all we come into contact with the revelations of the Scriptures. In dealing with the subject of teaching, from an Old Testament perspective, the Bath Qol lifts teaching to a level of divination.

One of the many joys of dealing with teaching from an Old Testament ideology is that teaching is more of a calling by God,than merely some sort of occupation. So many times the teaching of Scripture is a process that is haphazardly done. The lack of preparation on behalf of the teacher and the lack of interest and enthusiasm on the student's behalf have made biblical teaching seem somewhat out of date and melancholy. But the Old Testament reminds us that to be able to teach Scripture is a gift which has been given to us by God. The teachers are the receivers of God's word. The teachers are the conveyor belts that feed God's word to God's people. The biblical teacher is the one who has heard the sacred Bath Qol and has committed himself/herself to taking on the chore of feeding God's sheet the gospel. With the zeal of the Old Testament teachers, those who have committed themselves to rightfully dividing the word of truth have embarked on a beautiful and fruitful journey. Therefore, every step taken to fulfill their call should be taken seriously.

In the Old Testament, teaching was the response to God's call.When Isaiah responded to God's call, he went about teaching/preaching God's word, as given to him through the Bath Qol. When Jeremiah stood at the gates of Jerusalem and expounded on what God had told him, it was in response to the divine Bath Qol that had taken place while he was in his mother's womb. These Old Testament prophets, like many others, were teachers who had been called by God. Their reason for teaching derived from the Bath Qol, which meant that they had to have a deep level of commitment. Everyday their job consisted of teaching God's word to all those with whom they came into contact.

TEACHING FROM A NEW TESTAMENT PERSPECTIVE

With Jesus, teaching was an essential tool in spreading the Kerygma, or the good news of the gospel. In Matthew 4:23, Matthew records Jesus as one going about Galilee teaching the people the good news. Along with this homiletic skill, Jesus employed his teaching skills to help those with whom he came into contact, and to with, understand exactly what it meant to follow his teaching.

With his parable in Matthew 13:1-16, Jesus tells the Disciples that the Word of God has to take root in one's heart. The "good soil" is the heart that has been made fertile by Christ's teaching. The heart is tilled by the revelations and Scriptural understanding Christ brings to the ears and minds of the listeners. The "stony ground" is not simply an individual's coldness, which rejects the Word of God. The "stony ground" also refers to those who hear the Word of God without any teaching. Without teaching there is no understanding. The Word of God without understanding cannot penetrate a stony heart. A stony heart that has not been tilled with teaching, disallows understanding and growth. In keeping with the parable of the sower, this concept can be summed as, "Planting without teaching, will lead to a harvest of misunderstanding."

From reading the records of Jesus' ministry, as recorded in the Synoptic Gospels, it is quite evident that Jesus insisted on teaching every chance he got. In Matthew 21:37, Jesus was "teaching in the temple." The concepts Jesus brought to the ears of those who listened to him were so strange that it required a period of teaching. The good news that Christ shared among the rigid Jews, the baffling Disciples, and the religiously inexperienced Gentile went against all human reasoning. When Jesus told the people that to be Christ-like meant that they were to love everyone, including their enemies, he knew that a great deal of teaching and paradigms would have to go along with his words. In the fifth chapter of Matthew, Jesus sat down and taught the multitude what following Christ would entail. In each of the Beatitudes Jesus touched the tapes in every listener's heart. Whether their discomfort was a broken heart, inferiority, or peace maker, Jesus assured them in his teaching that God had already blessed them. For the poor, down trodden multitude to understand that even in their present stage/condition, required more than the preaching of the Word. There was also the need for teaching.

The proclamation of the Word was often followed by teaching methods that helped the Disciples and other followers not only hear but understand the teaching of Christ. Not only does Jesus teach the people, but he does it in their surrounding, the synagogue. In the 28th chapter of Matthew, Jesus gives those who have committed themselves to following his teachings, one of the greatest charges ever recorded in history. Jesus admonishes his followers to "Go ye therefore, and teach all nations, baptizing them in the name of the Father, and of the Son, and of the Holy Ghost: Teaching them to observe all things whatsoever I have commanded you" (Matthew 28:19-20a). Jesus did not simply tell the Disciples to go and share their views with the word. Neither did Jesus casually request the Disciples to preach. Rather, Jesus made sure that the Disciples understood that they were about to embark on the greatest adventure of their lives, which was undertaking the task of educating and enlightening the people on the teaching of Christ. With this charge, the Disciples were faithfully given the order to expound on Jesus' teaching with all they come into contact with. The Disciples' commission was to develop ways the Word of God could reach the minds and hearts of all humans.

NEW TESTAMENT TEACHING VERSUS PLURALISM

In looking at the passage of Scripture, it seems as if Jesus' idea of teaching was to be no less than what was considered customary or traditional Judaic community. Within the Judaic community, one was taught the Judaic laws and customs, during their childhood years. In every entity of the Judaic life, God's words to the people and their relationship with God was studied constantly. When the rich young ruler came to Jesus asking, "What must I do to inherit eternal life?" (Matt. 19:16-22) Jesus told him to keep the commandments. Notice that the young man immediately asserted that he had kept them from his youth to his present age. The young ruler had been taught the commandments. It was in his culture; his heritage; and his personal life. This is teaching! What the rich young ruler had undergone were extensive teaching periods. Nevertheless, the teaching was done within a community that accepted, agreed upon, and practiced the same principles.

But Jesus knew that teaching the gospel would require meeting opposition. When Jesus instructed the Disciples to go into all the corners of the world known to them, Jesus knew that the Disciples would encounter other religious and social doctrine which would not be parallel to the gospel. Nevertheless, he instructed them to go and teach. Jesus acknowledged that there were other doctrines, but he refused to limit his teaching to pacify those doctrines.

As Christians living in a world of pluralism and in society where anything and everything is accepted by one group or another, it is important that our teaching of Christ is not compromised with today's trend. In today's world, biblical teaching is accompanied by scientific theories and social ethics of various social groups. No longer is the word of God simply read by the teacher and understood by the students. The average teenage Bible student has been influenced by the media and the music industry. What was once outlawed and forbidden for the media to show, children can now see on daytime television. Words that were at one time banned by the FCC are being shouted through walkman earphones and into the minds of children. So much has changed! So much as happened since the last time the family gathered at the family's household altar. In homes where prayer was a family tradition, the altar has been replaced with a bar and stool set. The family's Bible that once laid on the living room table, with its leaves sprawled open for anyone and everyone to read has been replaced by an imported vase. To say that we have not witnessed these changes in some way or another would be nothing more than deceit. We understand why America is called "the melting pot". A lot of tradition and religion has been transformed to include other ways of living and thinking. But the gospel has not changed. The teacher who takes on the task of sharing God's word must do it in an uncompromising manner. This does not mean that the teacher is to be forceful or dogmatic. On the contrary, even in the planning stages of the class, the teacher must take into account that most of the students who will gather for class, regardless of their age, have experienced some levels of diversity.

It is when the teacher takes these matter into account and designs a curriculum that avoids diversity and at the same time create a lukewarm gospel that tips around the social conditions our people are experiencing. In the book, *Preaching In Times Like These*, George Buttrick contends that we should not attempt to keep the gospel in a bubble of utopia while the world undergoes all forms of tragedy.

Buttrick states, "Human nature and life's experiences are one. The wise man accepts them as one, but the foolish man tries to separate them. He is a fool swinging an ax frantically; chopping off his own toes." When we hide the gospel from the real world, we are cutting off our blessings. We are prohibiting our faith from witnessing the manifestation of God's word.

The gospel confronts us wherever we are. Regardless of our denomination or religion, the gospel of Jesus Christ is real. On the other hand, when the teacher commits to designing a curriculum that recognizes our diverse and pluralistic society and at the same time presents a Christocentric focus, learning and soul strengthening can take place. Go ahead and confront the social issues that are staring our sisters and brothers in the face. But while doing that, don't forget to teach a living Christ. Every teacher should develop a structure that addresses diversity; respect diversity; and feeds the kerygma to the students.

THE BIBLE AND THE TEACHER

It is imperative that biblical teachers understand that the gospel was not written so that it could be used as a defense against a pluralistic, twentieth century society. The Bible is not a defense mechanism designed to ward off the evils of cults, polytheism, nor any other religious or social entity. The Bible is the written wisdom of God's people which reveals to us: (1) the way the Old Testament character viewed God and (2) The good news of the gospel brought to humankind by Jesus.

To say that the Bible is a religious book and an authoritative source of truth is not to deny, of course, that it is also a very human book. From its pages we catch the voice of authentic human experiences. The teacher who searches the Bible for unique characteristics should remember that the Bible was written by and about people who tended cattle and struggled to raise their children in the paths of righteousness. These same people were happy and frightened, sometimes filled with faith and at other times with doubt. To miss the humanness of the pages of the Bible is to teach the Bible as a superficial piece of literature. The authenticity of the Bible does not depend on what other circles of beliefs say. Rather, the Bible stands as the recorded word of God, which was pre-ordained before the beginning of time. Biblical teaching should center around these ideals and focus on enlightening the student's path to wisdom, rather than debating on authenticity. Yes, our environment is changing rapidly, but the truth of God's word is still the same. God's word carries the same meaning today, as it did thousands of years ago. The teacher that uses the Bible to speak to contemporary issues has to first root himself/herself in the faith that the word of God was written then, but it also speaks now. The Bible is more than a record of God's action in history. It is also a paradigm of what God will do for us. Solid biblical teaching does not attempt to go around this. Solid biblical teaching uses this as its foundation.

How we teach the Bible depends partly on how we view the book that we teach. Some failures in Bible teaching stem from inadequate conceptions of the Bible itself. As we prepare to go into the next chapter on "Training Methods," it is imperative that we concentrate on the teacher's approach to the Bible, because the conception the teacher has is the view he/she will attempt to pass on to the students. The teacher is the foundation, and if the foundation is weak, so will everything that will be built on it. Too often, those who decide to teach from the biblical perspective simply grab the Bible without coming to some type of understanding as to what the book they are grabbing means to them. If the teacher does not have a clear understanding of what the Bible means to him/her, teaching without convictions will take place. And we all know that teaching without convictions, brings about no positive changes nor understanding. On the other hand, when the teacher teaches from the viewpoint that what he/she is sharing with the class is authentic, as well as contemporary, incarnate teaching and learning can take place. Incarnate teaching/learning is when what is being shared comes to life. Not only do the students read it an visualize it, but they also feel it.

After the teacher has decided to take on the awesome task of teaching God's word, he/she must then decide what methods will be used to reach the ears and minds of the students. This is an important decision because the success of biblical teaching does not rest on how much the teacher knows. Rather, the success depends on how well the teacher communicates or relays his/her interpretation of the studied text to the students.

Good Bible study always carries the ingredients of structure and methods. Often enough, teachers mistakenly assume that if their class consists of one of the ingredients, it will automatically have the other. But this is not necessarily true. Structure is the format, or design the teacher has chosen for the class. The structure consists of an outline of topics that will lead the Bible class to accomplishing the goals the teacher has set for the class. On the other hand, the methodical process involves the teacher who decides/develops ways that will insure and enhance the Bible class' movement from one level of understanding to another. As technical as these two terms may sound, Bible study with structure and method is what creates an informative, as well as a spiritual encounter between the teacher and the class. Teachers should always be mindful that unguided discussions about the Bible can be inefficient and disorganized, and are usually lacking in substance. With today's call for

Discipleship there still exists the need for structured Bible classes with appropriate methods, which fabricates a Bible study that fulfills the spiritual hunger of those who gather to learn God's word.

Conveying the interpreted word to the students is a challenge that requires the teacher to put on the principle of Hermeneutics, and decide the method of communication he/she will use to convey his/her understanding/interpretation to the students. Hermeneutics is a tool used to decipher the meaning of a work. Actually, it is a method of literary criticism that creates a process of understanding the meaning of work. Although many teachers may not understand the technical term hermeneutics, it is something every teacher does, in order to bring to life the meaning of ancient writing. In any class, there is already in existence a gulf between the students' ears and the teachers' understanding of Scripture. But what is also important for the teacher to understand is that the interpretation of Scripture is not the final point. The gruesome, yet rewarding challenge, is for the teacher to adequately share the findings of the studied passage with the students.

The thought of students relying on the interpretation of the teacher may generate some uneasy feelings within the teacher. While this is a tremendous burden for the teacher to carry, it is exactly what the teacher is expected to do. In everything we do we interpret! Our world is built on human's interpretation of what a society should be and how it should look. In every facet of life there is interpretation. Along with interpretation there is the biblical teacher's job description of conveying his/her interpretation to the class. The teacher should never shy away from extending to the class his/her studied, researched, and factual interpretation. After all, the teachers' interpretation is half of what Bible study is all about.

The teaching methods are what bridge the gap. The strength of the bridge depends greatly on the teaching methods the teacher decides to use. What types of methods should a teacher use? For the most part, it is for the teacher to decide as to what methods will be used. Nevertheless, good teaching skills compel the teacher to avoid methods which are full of social dogma rather than scriptural truth. Good teaching methods are designed to enlighten students and the teacher. Any teaching method that does not lift this concept is not worth bringing into the class. Along with the teacher's interpretation there should always remain room for other view points. Of course the teacher should be well prepared with a structural analysis of the studied passage of Scripture. But if the study time is to be a period of enlightenment, diverse thinking and input from others have to be encouraged and respected. When the view points of others are denied by teaching methods that feed information to the students, but do not allow the students to feed back into the class, the chance for biblical enlightenment is lost. Where there is no enlightenment, learning has not taken place; and if there is no chance of learning, then there is no need for the class to assemble.

SELECTING COMPATIBLE METHODS

The phrase "compatible methods" are methods that fit the styles of the teacher. Every teacher has idiosyncrasies which he/she brings into the classroom, and the styles or methods of teaching should be paralleled to these styles. In other words, the teaching methods the teacher chooses inside the classroom, should coincide with the styles that surround the teacher outside the classroom. When the teacher stays with methods that compliment his/her personal styles, the teaching becomes authentic, rather than something manufactured out of a teacher's manual. This is especially true with youth and young adults! It seems as if the younger generation can easily distinguish between the authentic and the manufactured. The teaching methods that hold the attention of the listeners are methods that allow the teacher to be real. Choosing methods that do not adequately support the teacher's personality, is like David trying to wear Saul's armor, when he was about to fight Goliath (I Sam. 17:38-39). The armor was excellent for Saul, but it did absolutely nothing for David, because the Blacksmith did not shape the armor with David in mind. The armor was made for Sau and Saul only. A lot of the teaching methods that are circulating through today's Bible class were not made with certain teachers in mind. Teachers who arbitrarily put on various teaching methods without considering it compatibility to their personal style, are trying to wear armor that was not made to fit them.

TEACHING METHODS EQUAL GOALS

Within the realms of structured teaching are goals set b the teacher. In order to have a clear understanding of wha is expected out of the class and the teacher, there should be set of goals the teacher and the class can follow (goal setting will be discussed in a later chapter). Once the goals of the class are set, the teacher can choose the teaching methods that will give the best assistance in accomplishing the goals. This is why it is imperative for the teacher to constructively design a curriculum which includes goal setting. Without the goals, the teacher cannot adequately decide as to what teaching methods would be most beneficial for the class. If the teacher does not know which direction he/she wants to lead the class (goal setting), then there is no need for deciding on teaching methods, because even the best teaching cannot steer a class. They can help the teacher steer the class, but teaching methods are not a substitute for effective planning and goal setting.

INDUCTIVE STUDY METHODS

For the most part, inductive Bible study falls within a broad category of approaches to teaching which emphasis the process of careful and controlled enlightenment. In inductive Bible studies the teacher and the students probe a certain passage in a careful and thorough manner. The teacher and students do not haphazardly take a passage of Scripture and affix some theological jargon to it. Through the use of the inductive methods, the teacher and the students give the author and the setting its full respect by taking into account the details and facts behind the passages. The inductive method analyzes the sitz-im-leben (the setting in life, or life situation). It helps the students and teacher bring to life the meaning of texts written thousands of years ago.

INDUCTIVE METHOD AS A SCIENTIFIC APPROACH

When inductive Bible study is referred to as scientific, it simply means that it follows the order of the scientific method of inquiry. Notice that the scientific methods begin with observation, rather than opinion. So does the inductive methods of Bible study. The scientist forms a hypothesis that best explains an observation and then designs an experiment to test it. In a similar way, the Bible study teacher and class form an interpretation based on careful observation of a text and then test the validity of that interpretation with other members of the group. Like the scientific method, the inductive method seeks to base its interpretation (hypotheses) on careful observation of the Bible (data) and not merely on opinions and conjecture. In other words, the teacher and the class become the Sherlock Holmes of biblical students. The teacher and the class form conclusions from the insights given by one another.

Now, this is not to say that the Bible study is merely scientific analysis dressed in exegetical garb. Unlike the scientific methods, the inductive method does not give the student a sense of being detached, impersonal, or superficial. The student is involved with the biblical passage so much so that he/she becomes a part of the living word and its world. The studied passage speaks to the student in the author's voice, and in the author's world. In essence, inductive Bible study does not claim to be a science, but rather it is a form of biblical study which shares with the scientific method the urge to test interpretations against facts rather than mere opinions.

IMPLEMENTING INDUCTIVE BIBLE STUDY

Good inductive Bible study takes place in a small group that is not dominated by one person. Inductive study consists of small study groups and makes use of discussion, but the biblical approach that the teacher and the students make is unique. The inductive method consists of three distinct steps or ingredients. They are observation/description, interpretation, and application. Each is designed to accomplish part of the process of understanding a passage of Scripture. Within the inductive process, small groups collectively study Scripture with little intervention from the teacher. With this process, all group members can share their ideas, ask questions, and seek help in clearing up diverse opinions and ideas about a certain passage. The incentive in the inductive method is the small groups and the personal time of interaction. Also, by the teacher having little input during small group time, the students get to focus on their findings, instead of the teacher's pre-planned outline.

Also, inductive study reaches its greatest potential with small groups because it pushes for one hundred percent participation. Discussion, brainstorming, and debating questions back and forth can all be part of an inductive Bible study. Actually inductive Bible study serves notice to the participants that the Bible study class will not be a spectator's event! Inductive Bible study encourages everyone to participate. Participation from the entire class means that enlightenment or biblical discoveries will be accomplished with the teacher and class functioning as a community. All of these elements are what makes inductive Bible study methods motivating pieces in today's Bible class.

GROUP ACTIVITIES: AN APPROACH TO INDUCTIVE BIBLE STUDY

Since the inductive study method is used with small groups, the teacher has an excellent chance of expounding on the lesson through the use of group activities. With the group being small, group activities can be done with one group, rather than the class breaking up into several groups. This really helps the class and the teacher analyze the text in more of a communal atmosphere, because the teacher does not have to worry about combating and facilitating different concepts from groups sprawled out across the classroom. In any Bible study, the teacher wants feedback from the class, and the small group atmosphere fosters this concept better than the large group model. In a large group setting, the teacher either has to go around to each group, or wait for general assembly to respond. Of course there will be different ideas within the one group, but with the teacher working with one group. there is time for the teacher to respond to the different ideas, answers, and conclusions while group discussion is in progress.

GROUP QUESTIONS AS A METHOD

A stimulating activity for small groups is writing questions. In this activity the group, as a whole, agree on questions they feel are pertinent to the text. This activity evokes group discussion, because it impels the students and the teacher to communicate with one another. When the questions are written down by a designated person, the group takes a minimal break (students and teacher need time to change from the role of looking only at the text for questions to searching for answers); reassemble with the teacher opening and leading the discussion. Although this i a group activity, the teacher should at all times remain as the leader of the discussion. Why? First of all, when there is a group discussion, the focus sometimes becomes distorted with unrelated topics, people taking a long time to give a short answer, opinionated views rather than facts, and other common distractions found in Bible study groups. The teacher has to guide the discussion, while at the same time address the questions, because the teacher knows that the most effective questions concentrate on the vital aspects of the passage. The group has derived the questions from the passage of Scripture, but the teacher is the one who guides the students in their discovery of the Bible's message.

Also, we must keep in mind that prior to class time, the well trained teacher has developed his/her interpretation or understanding of the passage, and the teacher's job is to share with the class his/her insights. With the pre-developed goals in mind, the teacher can address the questions; hear from the other students; and guide the discussion along with his/her input. It is critical that the teacher does not present his/her insights as the overall precise answer, for this will make the students withhold their thoughts. With pre-planned goals and thorough preparation of the studied passage, the teacher should not have any trouble weaving his/her insights into the class, without dominating it.

COACH-PLAYER METHOD

With the coach-player model, the Bible teacher takes on the role of the coach and the students take on the role of the team players. The teach (coach) gives the students (players) bits and pieces of information about the studied passage. The teacher (coach) enables the students by giving them information and guides them (with personal input, from time to time) to making their own biblical discoveries. The class takes on the role of the team players by following the teacher's lead. Just as the team players are the ones who make the plays an score the points, the students follow the lead of the coach/teacher and bring to light the discoveries of the passage. Just as a coach designs the plays for the team to follow, the teacher designs the outline the class is to follow. The teacher does not have to show the outline to the class, but he/she should make sure the team follows the outline. This way, verbal scattering and other distractions can be avoided. The teacher makes sure the class stays with the outline by interjecting topics and ideas for the class to expound on. In this model, the teacher, acting as coach only facilitates the class. Although the teacher's role is still that of a leader, the main emphasis is on the players. The students, like the team players, are the main action characters. The players follow the plays and score the points by bringing to life the passage and by developing a thorough understanding/interpretation of the passage.

This model works well with small groups, but the teacher must be on guard. With this method, there is plenty of room for freestyle exegeting. By simply letting the players dominate the activity, the teacher can easily loose sight of the pre-planned goals, which are essential for nourishing Bible study. Just as the coach cannot afford to let the players run the team, the teacher cannot afford to let the students take over the class. With this model, the teacher has to make it clear to the participants their role as players. And throughout the Bible study, the teacher must remember his/her role as coach. As players, the students make the observations, interpretations, and apply it to today's world The teacher's role is only to lead and assist. Remember, the coach's presence can manifest on the playing field, but the coach is not allowed on the playing field.

THE DIRECTED METHOD

Like the inductive method, the directed method is based on the same methodology of observation, interpretation, and application. The differentiating factor of directed study is that this method replaces group discovery with the leader's sharing of his/her insights into a passage. As noted earlier in the discussion of inductive study, the teacher gives insight, but the teacher is not the main focus. The discussion in inductive study is more group oriented. With directed study, the teacher does most of the talking, while the class takes notes. This is not to say that in directed study the teacher does all the talking. The teacher asks questions which are intended to lead students in uncovering the facts of the passage. In both approaches, the teacher is the central figure. But in the directed study, the teacher mainly feeds the students, rather than the students and teachers sharing insights with one another.

USING THE DIRECTED METHOD

Usually when the Bible study group makes up a large assembly, the directed method is the best approach. The larger the gathering, the harder it is for the teacher to work on a small group basis. Individually sharing would take up most of the class time, so the teacher needs to use the method that walks the students through the observation, interpretation, and application process. Also, if a group is made up of new comers, recently converted members, or youth members, teacher should probably take a more directed approach. In situations such as these, it is best that the teacher instructs, rather than a group leader. With newcomers to the church and/or to Christ, the intake of information is a delicate process. Whatever is taught to the "babes in Christ," this information will have an effect on them for the rest of their life.The teacher has to make sure that what is being fed to the newcomers is not only correct, but spiritually digestible. In settings such as the ones discussed, the directed method does not waste time on breaking into small groups, because there would be too many groups and too little results. If a large group were to assemble into small groups, the teacher would have to break himself/herself into hundreds of pieces to adequately tend to the data and feedback a large assembly would generate. In every respect the teacher needs to always be in control of the class. The more groups an assembly breaks into, the less chance the teacher will have of controlling the class and its time. On the other hand, directed Bible study allows the teacher, who is skilled in Bible teaching to teach the Bible in an atmosphere conductive to learning.

With the directed method, the teacher can "open the passage" for the class by sharing the facts (not mere opinions) in outline form. Outline form of presentation is recommended by Bible teachers, because the outline form prevents the teacher from scattering. The teacher's train of thought can flow in a structured manner, which makes it easier for the students to comprehend. Also, the outline form of presentation supports the teacher as the main character. To every skilled Bible teacher, the questions and insights of the students are important and should be welcomed. And this is one of the advantages of the outline form. With the outline form the questions are directed to the teacher (main character) and the teacher shares the interpretation/understanding his/her research has revealed. Developing and teaching from an outline will be discussed in a later chapter.

Chapter 3
Teaching the Teacher

This section focuses on the training of teachers for Christian discipleship. Why teachers' training? Because teaching disciples (students) is the primary responsibility of Christian discipleship. The Great Commission, Matthew 28:19, says:

> Go ye therefore, and teach all nations, baptizing them in the name of the Father, and of the Son, and of the Holy Ghost. Teaching them to observe all things whatsoever I have commanded you: and , lo, I am with you always, even unto the end of the world. Amen.

The Revised Standard Version and New International Version translate this passage as to "make disciple."

> Go therefore and make disciples of all nations, baptizing them in the name of the Father and of the Son and of the Holy Spirit, teaching them to observe all that I have commanded you; and lo, I am with you always, to the close of the age. (Matthew 28:19 RSV)

The word "teach" is translated "make disciple" because the Greek word that is used for "teach" is "matheteuo", which literally means "to become a student" or "enroll as a scholar." It could also be translated as 'to teach or to instruct one who has become a student." The passage could possible be translated as "Go therefore and teach everyone who want to become my student ...."

Disciple means being a student or scholar of a particular teacher or teaching. One learns the teaching of the teacher by literally following behind the teacher. Not only does one learn by precept (intellectually), but also one learns by example (emotionally, psychologically and empirically: practice -learning by doing). From the New Tesament we find the teaching and training of a disciple were holistic approaches. Therefore, the mandate and commission of the church are to teach persons to become students and scholars of Jesus and his teaching. It is of paramount concern and job No.1 that the local church teach teachers to teach. As Jesus said, "Follow me and I will make (qualify) you to become fishers of men" (Matthew 4:19).

Before beginning to the teach the teachers there are several questions that need to be answered and solutions that need to be explored:

1. What is going to be taught?
2. Who is going to be taught?
3. Who is going to teach?

Once these basic questions are answered, clarified and understood the training task is 50% completed.

WHAT TO TEACH

This question deals with designing a course of study or curriculum for teacher. The that question that should to be asked is, "What knowledge and skills should a person have if he/she is going to teach others to become students/disciples of Jesus? or "What qualifies one to be a teacher of Jesus' students/disciples?" If one reviews any State Department of Education curriculum for certifying teachers one will find some basic courses that are universal. That is, there are some basic concepts that any good teacher should and ought to know (e.g. Math, History, English, Psychology, Philosophy, Education, teaching methods etc.). Let us consider some basic concepts that a teacher of Jesus students/disciples should know.

1. It should be obvious that any teacher who is going to teach students of Jesus ought to themselves first know Jesus. This is pertinent because often teachers are selected to teach in the church without first considering whether or not they themselves are students/disciple of Jesus. The teacher of Jesus' students/disciples cannot teach without being a student. So the teacher is a student/teacher or a learner/teacher. The following questions should be asked:

a. Is the potential teacher already studious in learning more about Jesus in order to become like Jesus?

b. Does the potential teacher engage in regular prayer and Bible study both in private (at home) and in church (group study sessions)?

These questions are essential because a student/disciple's final graduation from Jesus' school of discipleship will not commence until the Resurrection.

2. Teachers of Jesus' students/disciples should follow the living Word. The living word is Jesus. The teacher should have a personal relationship with Jesus. As Guy P. Leavitt states: "...you teach most by what you are" (*Teach With Success* page 13). And more specifically, you teach by who you are. Having a personal relationship with Christ means that you have become a new creature (Colossians 3:1). It is this new creature that the students should come to know,

trust and follow. As the students learn and follow you, you should be learning and following Jesus.

How should a teacher follow Jesus? J. M. Price in "*Jesus The Teacher*," suggests several qualifications which made Jesus the ideal teacher and which a good teacher should strive to follow.

Jesus embodied the truth. He said: "I am the way, the truth and the life." (John 14.6). Price notes that Jesus "...was 100 percent what he taught." He incarnated truth from the overflow of his life. Quoting S. D. Gordon, Price continues, "Jesus was before he did, he lived what he taught, and lived it before he taught it, and live it far more that he could teach it" (Price, page10).Price further explains that Jesus' incarnation of truth grew out of two things. "One was that he was God and possessed in perfection the qualities of God. He was the only perfect being" (page10). Secondly, "his embodiment of the truth grew out of the fact the he studied and experienced it, and made it a part of himself" (Price, page 10).

Price also suggests that Jesus' embodiment of the truth affected his teaching in at least two ways. (1) The truth gave Jesus' teaching a note of authority. Especially, since truth nor authority was found in the teaching of the scribes, rabbis nor the official teachers. We read in Mark 1:22, "And they were astonished at his doctrine: for he taught them as one that had authority, and not as the scribes." Jesus' teaching was from within. Secondly, Jesus "...living what he taught also inspired confidence in his statement" (Price, page 11). There was consistency in what Jesus taught and practiced and people trusted him. "They observed how he experienced sorrow, criticism, disappointment and persecution. His living reinforced and gave weight to what he said, 'The greatest thing the disciples got from his teaching was not a doctrine but an influence. To the last hour of their lives the big thing was that they had been with him" (Price, page 11).

Price points out that the desire to serve is another quality that the teacher who follows Jesus must possess. Without the desire to serve, Price concludes, a teacher is but a "sounding brass or a tinkling cymbal" (Price, page 11). Jesus was truly interested in people. He came to heal and liberate broken and hurting humanity. He said:

> The Spirit of the Lord is upon me, because he hath anointed me to preach the gospel to the poor, he hath sent me to heal the brokenhearted, to preach deliverance to the captives, and recovering of sight to the blind, to set at liberty them that are bruised, To preach the acceptable year of the Lord (Luke 4:18-19).

Jesus was compassionate. And every good teacher who follows Jesus should be compassionate. As Price states (Price, page 13):

> This attitude has characterized every great teacher through the ages - Pantaenus as he started the first Christian school at Alexandria alongside a pagan university; Benedict as he organized a teaching order at Monte Cassino that influenced Europe for three centuries; Gerard Groote as he founded the Brothers of the Common Life to teach poor children; Loyola as he constituted the Jesuit order to teach youth; and Robert Raikes as he started the Sunday School movement which has gone around the world.

Another characteristic cited by Price, which teachers should strive to emulate, is that Jesus sought to form right ideals. For Jesus right and "proper knowledge is necessary to proper living. One cannot live much better than he knows.

Right conduct is rooted in right understanding" (page 40). These ideals are expressed in Jesus' attitudinal teaching called the "Beatitudes" Matthew 5:1-12. Teachers of ideals and attitudes clearly understand that as a student "...thinketh in his heart, so is he" (Proverb 23:7). Jesus, the teacher, was clearly focused on his objective, to"...be about his Father's business." With that in mind Jesus' task as a teacher was to relate persons properly to God. He said to Nicodemus, "Unless you are born again..." (John 3:3, Living Bible). Therefore, the attitude winning others to Christ should be a good teacher's joy and hope.

3. The student/teacher who is following Jesus needs to know the Bible (the written Word). Basic knowledge about the history, books, and the division of the Bible is imperative for the teacher. The teacher should be acquainted with general information of authorship, date, and purpose of writing, including theological and doctrinal truths. By understanding the theological and doctrinal truths the student/teacher will be able to focus on the primary thought and message, that is ageless and timeless. These theological and doctrinal truths come from God. Hence, the teacher need to know what "Thus saith the Lord God....." (Ezekiel 3:11a). Because the truth that God spoke yesterday is good today and will be good tomorrow.

The student/teacher who recognizes the importance of study and preparation from a Biblical perspective will strive to build a home/personal library of Bible commentaries, Bible dictionaries, concordances and Biblical maps. Since the student/teacher is building minds and souls, these are tools that must become familiar and useful.

Above all, understanding the written Word comes from Divine insight and wisdom. Meditation and prayer cannot be usurped by any amount of reading from commentaries or dictionaries. The teacher is not just imparting knowledge but teaching the words of persons who were inspired by God.

The teacher should be inspired to teach. Only the Holy Spirit can make the teaching come alive and meaningful. Pray, pray and continue to pray for the Holy Spirit is the teacher's teacher (John 13:).

KNOW THE CHURCH

God has called the church to be the instrument and means of grace through which Jesus manifests his teaching and presence to a dying world. The primary arena for Christian teaching is within the church. To know the church, its origin, history, purpose and organizational structure is as important to know as the company or business for which you work. There are general church history and theology of which the student/teacher must be aware (e.g. the history of the Christian Church, the Apostolic Fathers, the Protestant Reformation, Sects etc.). However, not only should the student/teacher have some knowledge of the history of Christianity, but he/she should know as much as possible about the history of their own local church or congregation. The history of the local church should be in continuum with the history of Jesus, the founder, author and finisher of the church (Matthew16:18).

KNOW THE STUDENT

Jesus the, model teacher, knew his disciples (students). He knew their strengths, weaknesses, talents and faults. Following Jesus' example in knowing the student will enable the student/teacher to establish a bonding relationship where both teacher and students share knowledge and information together and learn from each other.

This is why Richard E. Rusbuldt in *Basic Teacher Skills* describes teaching as a "two-way communication" (Rusbuldt, page 30). And he identifies some of the teacher's roles as communicator, facilitator, and translator (Rusbuldt, page 35). The teaching/learning experience, in essence for Rusbuldt is sharing and caring. He calls it the heart of teaching (Rusbuldt, page 40-41). The sharing teacher shares:

THE STORY
MY STORY
CONTENT
PLANS
RELATIONSHIPS
HOPES AND DREAMS
HONESTY
LIFE
TRUTH

The caring teacher expresses care through:

FEELINGS
LISTENING
OBSERVING
SENSING
RELATING
CRYING
CHEERING
PRAYING

And the student who is blessed to have such a teacher shares and cares with the teacher, but also in return exhibits sharing and caring in life settings.

Hence, the student/teacher will endeavor to know and understand age level characteristics. Leavitt (Guy P. Leavitt, *Teach with Success*, page 33-41) gives a brief description of age levels characteristics and how the function and interact in the teaching/learning experience.

Crib Babies - Birth to One Year

General Characteristics

Tiny, dependent upon adults to meet needs, cries to communicate needs, requires individual attention, sleeps a great deal, learns by the attitudes of those around him.

Toddler - Age One

General Characteristics

Constanly moving, learning to talk, learning through all five senses, limited vocabulary, imitative in action, attention span of no more than two minutes, requires individual attention, learning to be with other children, fearful, tires easly.

Ages Two and Three

General Characteristics

Extremely active, attention span of three to five minutes, responds to guided play, rapidly growing vocabulary (although still limited), imitative in actions and speech, learns through all five senses, susceptible to disease, tires easily, achieving physiological stability, forming simple concepts of social reality, learning to distinguish right and wrong behavior, curious, learns by repetition, plays alongside others rather than with them, feels the love in a Christian atmosphere.

Beginner - Ages Four and Five

General Characteristics

Very active, imitators, attention span of five to ten minutes, enjoys playing with other children, forming concepts of social and physical reality, inquisitive, learning to relate to adults rather than parents, big imagination, developing sense of right and wrong, learning to share, tires easily, growing vocabulary, curious, thinks of God in personal terms, responds to Jesus with simple trust.

Level of Understanding
Knows God created the world, loves Jesus, and wants to see Him pleased. thinks church is a happy, special place to go, willing to work with others, eager to help, shares, learns Bible words, invites others to come to Bible school.

Primary - Grades One and Two
General Characteristics
Active, talkative, imaginative, likes group activities, asks questions, seeks personal attention from the teacher, small muscles developing, builing attitudes toward himself, learning masculine or feminine role, learning to read and write,
developiong conscience and sense of morality, thinks concretely, honest, eager to learn, emotionally immature, attention span of seven to fifteen minutes.

Level of Understanding
Appreciates the Bible as a special book, genuinely loves God and Jesus, prays sincerely, understands that Jesus is a special person, beginning to understand what sin is, can apply the Bible principles to everyday problems.

Middler - Grades Three and Four
General Characteristics
Energetic, healthy, thinks concretely, likes group activities, asks questions, enjoys personal attention from the teacher and other adults, continues to build attitudes toward himself, begins to demonstrate specific interests, "law and order" sense of morality, emotionally immature, eager to learn, memorizes easily, wants to help, attention span of ten to fifteen minutes.

Level of Understanding

Chronologically understands the application of Bible principles to the problems, Jesus as Savior, sin, need for salvation.

Junior - Grades Five and Six
General Characteristics

Energetic, healthy, loud, inquisitive, talkative, imaginative, wants to be like his peers, beginning to think abstractly, has many interests, likes competition, hero worshipper, dislikes outward display of affection, gang spirit, wants to be involved in classroom procedure, "law and order" morality, memorizes easily, activities affected by attitudes toward himself, developing attitudes toward social groups and institutions, independent, attention span of ten to twenty minutes.

Level of Understanding

Chronologically understands what sin is, need for salvation, Jesus as Savior, Bible background, application of the Bible to daily problems.

Young Teen - Grades Seven, Eight, and Nine
General Characteristics

Awkward, growing rapidly, self-conscious, boisterous, independent, peer approval more important than adult approval, interested in the opposite sex, capable of abstract thinking, able to reason, developing his own faith and value system, definite interests and skills, increasing doubts.

Level of Understanding

Has an understanding and application of Biblical principles in life; what is sin is, Jesus as Savior, and interrelationship in Biblical material.

Senior High - Grades Ten, Eleven, and Twelve

General Characteristics

Independent, rapily increasing abilities, sometimes a "know-it-all," emotional, grown-up one day but a child the next, doubts, settling on his own value system and faith, physically mature, influenced by peer pressure, can reason well, interested in the opposite sex, thinks abstractly, choosing a vocation, cliquish.

Level of Understanding

Understands the following concepts: Christian lifestyle; life application of Biblical principles, relationship of the Bible to science, history, and literature, worship; what sin is; Jesus as Savior; interrelationship in Biblical material.

Young Adult - Ages Eighteen to Twenty-four

General Characteristics

Selecting a mate in learning to live as a single, establishing a home, completing education and/getting started in a vocation, settling into an adult faith, desiring a practical faith.

Level of Understanding

Finds the Bible a source of power; understands Jesus is Savior and Lord.

Adult

General Characteristics

Who are these adults? Those in their twenties differ from those in their thirties who differ from those in their forties. Those in their forties differ from those in their fifties. Those in their sixties differ still, as do those who are older. So no two adults are alike, although some psychosocial adjustments must be made by all adults: rearing children, accepting the changes of aging, advancing in a vocation, adjusting to aging parents, handling emotions of both a positive and negative nature, establishing affiliations with one's age group, learning to accept death.

Level of Understanding
Uses the Bible as a guide; understands Jesus as Savior and Lord

Knowing general characteristics, needs, and level of understanding the student will facilitate and enhance the learning experience. In addition, regular calling or visitation in the home and with the family of the student will make learning a personal and mutual venture.

WHO SHOULD BE TAUGHT

Everyone who is involved in a leadership or teaching role in the church should have a basic understanding of teaching skills. Leaders or officers of the church, by virture of their position are teachers (I Timothy 3:2). They teach through their methods and procedures of leadership. Discipleship teaching is a life style. We teach basically by who we are. However, there are no substitutes for the skills of a master teacher.

Regular teachers' training sessions should be a part of every church's program. Weekly training sessions or teaching meetings should be a requirement for Sunday School teachers and children and youth leaders, especially if youth groups meet once a week. There are some innovative ways to conduct teachers' training sessions. Sessions could be held before Bible study, choir practice, or Sunday School. A Saturday breakfast or luncheon could be designed for a training session. Through prayer and imagination a session could be developed to meet your need. You may even consider mass teaching for the entire congregation.

WHO SHOULD TEACH THE TEACHER

In most settings it will probably be suggested that the pastor should do the teaching. The pastor has a mandate and calling from God to preach and teach. And this responsibility should not be usurped. However, in some cases (extreme cases) this is not always feasible nor practical and a lay person may be called upon to teach and train the teachers. But even in those extreme cases the pastor should be the one who instructs, directs and guides the lay person is doing the teaching (Bishop E. Lynn Brown, *Pastor as Equipping Disciple*, page 45). The person who is doing the teaching should meet the same standards as described above for teachers. And even more so, this person should endeavor to attend workshops and training sessions, seminars and conferences for teachers. There is no substitute for a well prepared and well trained teacher who is going to teach teachers.

DEVOTION AND PRAYER

Pray, pray, and pray is the first act of preparation for the disciple/teacher. Jesus, the Master Teacher, frequently spent time in prayer and communication with God (Matt Friedeman, *The Master Plan of Teaching*). Prayer opens the pathway to Divine communication and allows the teaching, guiding, and leading of the Holy Spirit to teach the teacher. The Holy Spirit is the disciple/teacher's teacher. Jesus said, "...He will teach you all things, and bring to your remembrance all that I have said to you" (John 13: 26b). Through the solitude of devotion, the Holy Spirit prepares the heart and mind so that the disciple/teacher will give of his/her faith. It has been previously noted that true teachings come from within, and what "comes from the heart goes to the heart." A "heart felt" teaching and learning experience will surely bear fruit in the life of both teacher and student.

RESEARCH AND STUDY

Effective class room sessions require informed and informative teachers. The disciple/teacher is a student/teacher. The wise teacher is aware the he/she is also a student and must constantly study and grow in knowledge and grace of the Lord. Study means the good disciple/teacher will read and meditate on his/her lesson at a week before the class session (see Lesson Plan).

The conscientious disciple/teacher also recognizes the importance of research when preparing to teach. Research means learning and understanding the definition and pronunciation of new and unfamiliar words, or familiar words that have a different usage. Bible, dictionary, commentaries, encyclopedias should be the disciple/teacher's constant companion. The disciple/teacher should also read other related materials: novels, articles, newspaper, magazines, etc.

CLASSROOM APPEARANCE

The classroom appearance adds to or distracts from the learning experience. The classroom helps to establish the mood and atmosphere for learning. Leavitt (Leavitt, page 57-62). suggests several basic features of a classroom that promotes learning.

It should be clean regardless of the condition of the equipment. There is no excuse for an unclean, dingy, and musty classroom. The teacher is the caretaker of his/her classroom, and the appearance of the room conveys the attitude and disposition of the teacher. If the old saying, "cleanliness is next to godliness" is correct, then a clean and pleasant room will make the students have a sense of godliness. Juniors and older pupils can assist in the cleanliness of the classroom. The teacher can promote this action by having a clean-up and paint-up party. Keeping the room clean should be a routine classroom activity involving students of all ages.

The classroom should also be attractive. This added dimension does not mean going over board purchasing expensive materials. It can be as simple as a vase of flowers or plants appropriately placed. Fresh and attractive curtains along with bright colors used throughout the room can enhance the learning experience. In addition religious pictures, artifacts, posters, and bulletin boards can not only be useful for the appearance sake, but also as silent or subliminal tools to reinforce the objectives, main thought and other ideas concerning the lesson.

The classroom should be educationally arranged. Leavitt (Leavitt, page 57) suggests a rectangular room with a ratio of three feet in length and two feet in width. The look dimension, the outside walls and another solid unbroken wall with a window should provide the backdrop for the teacher to stand so that a light will not distract the pupils.

The classroom should be large enough to allow each pupil adequate space. The amount of adequate space for students is determined by age levels. The active preschooler requires more space than an adult. Crowding inhibits learning but too much space can be also be distractive and wasteful. Whatever the age level, space should be appropriate for comfortable classroom activity.

The classroom should be properly lighted. Too much light can be distractive and harmful as too little light. A specialist from the local electric or public utility company can be consulted for proper lighting level adjustments. Outside lighting can be regulated by curtains of blinds.

It should be properly ventilated and comfortable. A stuffy and stale room makes the mind feel dull. Fresh clean air provides adequate oxygen allowing the mind to function at its maximum intellectual level. However, on the other hand, too much of a breeze can be drafty and uncomfortable. A classroom that is environmentally prepared for learning will neither be too warm or too cold. This may not be always possible, but whatever can be done should be done to create an ideal learning environment.

The classroom should be free of noise. During the classroom sessions both teacher and student should be clearly heard and understood. Sound absorbing ceiling and wall material can help control distracting sound. Carpeting will modify and control noise especially in area where preschooler and primary children activities are conducted.

The classroom should have a sense of sacredness. Sacredness means that the classroom area is special. A place or area set-apart for a learning and nurturing time with the Lord. The sacredness of the room should be reflected in appearance (pictures, Bibles, mural, symbols, etc.) and in how the room is treated. As an area dedicated to the study of the Lord's, the room should be treated with divine love and care.

THE LESSON PLAN

The lesson plan states what the teacher intend to do during the class session. It is an outline or course of action of how the class will be conducted. Lesson plans are not necessarily always written. There are, however, several advantages to having a thorough carefully written lesson plan. (1) A well prepared lesson plan enables the disciple/teacher to envision the class session, noting what will happen, when it will happen, and what will be accomplished. The disciple/teacher can project subject material that should be highlighted or emphasized. (2) By preparing a lesson plan difficult areas and problems can be anticipated. This will enable adjustments and revisions to be made before the class begins. (3) A prepared lesson is helpful, useful, and almost a necessity, particularly for substitute teachers. The lesson plan enables the substitute teacher to maintain continuity with the subject material.

An effective lesson plan should include four basic parts:

(1) An objective, goal or aim
(2) Plan of presentation
(3) Materials)

(4) Evaluation

(1) Objective, goal or aim. The objective includes both knowledge of the students' interests, needs, and understanding of Scriptures, and the main thought or idea of the lesson material. From this the teacher develops the target, goal or purpose of his/her presentation. Leavitt suggests the following criteria for writing the objective, goal or aim (Leavitt, page 70):

A. Clear
B. Concise
C. Attainable
D. State in terms of pupil's behavior
E. Specific

The aim should also state what the student will learn, understand or do at the close of the class session.

The plan or method of presentation should be suitable to the student age level and the particular objective or aim of the lesson. The fundamentals for designing a plan of presentation are based on the two ways in which an individual learns. Leavitt defines the two methods thusly (Leavitt, page 79):

> One is by impression - that is, he/she sees, hears, smells, feels, or tastes - uses the senses.
> The other is by expression - he/she thinks, speaks, or acts.

The plan of presentation should use impression and expression activities and exercises in conducting the lesson. For more information see Chapter 2, "Teaching Methods."

Material is the resources that are going to be used during the class session. The lesson plan should identify books, maps, charts, articles, arts and crafts. Care and caution should be exercised to ensure age appropriateness and the ability of the material to reinforce the main idea or thought of the lesson.

Evaluation is as essential as the objective. Proper evaluation measures the students' retention and learning process. It reveals whether the goals or aims were reached as well as denoting the strength and weaknesses of the teacher and class presentation. An effective disciple/teacher uses the evaluation to make improvement and make adjustments for future class sessions.

Chapter 5
Developing Learning Skills

The Christian faith is a growth process by which we become new persons in Christ Jesus. It is a transformation of our being and lifestyle. Paul writes:

> Do not be conformed to this world: but be transformed by the renewal of your mind, that you may prove what is the will of God, what is good and acceptable and perfect (Romans 12:2, RSV).

This transformation is a learning experience - a learning experience which entails change. We learn by reflecting, doing, and being (Martha M. Leypoldt, *Learning is Change*, page 6). Reflection is the opportunity to reflect on experiences in our life and relate those experiences to current activity, Doing is the opportunity to participate in some kind of activity. Being is the state of awareness that we are in the process of becoming and that we have arrived.

Learning develops through the following activities (Leypoldt, page 25):

(1) Listening
(2) Responding
(3) Exploring
(4) Discovering
(5) Interpreting personal meaning

(6) Assuming responsibility

As we learn we become changed individuals. We are transformed, and our entire personhood is changed. And as one aspect of our being is changed, it affects other aspects, making us different persons. In the course of change our physical, mental, emotional, psychological, and spiritual entities are transformed.

There are three kinds of changes that are involved in making us new persons (Leypoldt, page 6):

(1) Knowing
(2) Feeling
(3) Doing

(1) When we learn our mind is changed by adding new information. Information that is learned can be recalled reacted to and an effort can be made to try to understand Understanding is the ability to apply experiences, analyze and evaluate.

(2) Learning is also changing our feelings about ideas things, persons, and circumstances. Feeling is attitude toward what is happening. It involves the sensitive awareness of ideas, persons, and things. It is valuing and making a commitment to values.

We learn basically at the feeling level. And new information is not accepted unless we are comfortable with it. If the new information evokes negative feelings we will not accept the new information until we are able to get beyond our negative feelings.

(3) Learning involves changing our actions. Changing our action may mean changing our way of doing things According to Leypoldt (page 29):

> Changes of actions are usually accomplished by following these certain steps:
> Being aware of possible alternative actions.
> Evaluating each alternative action.

Foreseeing consequences of each alternative.
Selecting an appropriate action on the basis of
a value system.
Assuming the responsibility of accepting the
consequences of new actions.

Leypoldt also identified several influences that tend to change persons. He states (Leypoldt page 57):

The following influences tend to change persons.
1. A person.
2. A group of persons.
3. Acquiring information
4. The use of resources.
5. An act of God: physical and/or spiritual.
6. Conditions conducive to learning.
7. The kind of approach made to people.
8. The kinds of feelings one has toward persons, situations, and self.
9. One's psychological makeup.
10. One spiritual sensitivity.
11. One's sensitivity to persons.
12. The degree of trust one has in persons.
13. The degree of trust one has in himself.
14. The degree of trust one has in God.

These influences are essential factors for Christian growth, which is a being, learning, doing, and changing experience. Jesus calls us to teach and he calls us to learn (Matthew 28:19; 10:29). Both are continuing processes and demanding challenges. Let us pray that the God of grace and God of glory will "...grant us wisdom and grant us courage for the facing of this hour" ("God of Grace and God of Glory," *The Book of Hymns*, page 470).

CONCLUSION

The learning/teaching process is a requirement of every one who would be a disciple of Jesus Christ. In terms of Christian discipleship, to learn and to teach what one has learned is a holistic lifestyle. Bishop Marshall Gilmore in his book *Discipleship in Principle and Practice* (page 8) states:

> Discipleship is the life embodied in human beings. They live out the life in every aspect of their lives. As the life lays claim on more and more of their beings, their witness to the life increases in its range of contacts. Thus, discipleship is being, but, by virtue of the fact that disciples are living creatures they do discipleship spontaneously. They may participate in planned activities but like their Lord, they minister as instruments of **the life** as they live, move and have their being. Discipleship, like the Spirit that gives it birth, functions where it wills. Like the Spirit the evidence is the fruit discipleship bears.

Learning and teaching discipleship is spontaneous life, which has being in the body of Christ. The body of Christ is the church, a community of Spirit that embodies the Spirit of Jesus Christ. Learning and teaching discipleship is being "in Christ." As clarified by Bishop Gilmore (page 54), he states:

> I suggest that to be "in Christ" as, "religious experience." means to participate in community. The "Christbody" is the immediate focus of community, but the fact that life is unitary means that the realization of its potential for community

is the work of discipleship. That is to be done from the community of faith with the community of faith acting in concert and/or through individual disciples and move into any one of several worlds to which disciples of Christ are related.

Churches that would engage in encounters that foster community, which means bringing life abundant to the family, the workplace, the marketplace, the place of leisure and recreation, the place of study, and the place of worship, must strive to become "communities that take time for the Spirit."

Bishop Gilmore defines this Spirit as the Spirit of love. He says:

Love is mutual self-giving in the body of Christ (John 13:35). Love is more than feeling. That is what Paul wrote to the Church at Corinth. He said, "Let all that you do be done in love" (I Cor. 16:14). Further, he told the Galatians what really counts "in Christ Jesus." He said, "the only thing that counts is faith working through love" (Gal. 5:6b).

Love is the agency that moves all things toward community. It expresses a uniqueness through and in discipleship. The uniqueness is a responsibility that Jesus taught his disciple. He said, Love your enemies..." (Luke 6:27). And, "If you love those who love you, what credit is that to you? For even sinners love those who love them" (6:32).

Discipleship learning/teaching, through the Spirit, within the community of faith, is a labor of love. It is with love that this book has been written. I hope that it is received with love and the thoughts, ideas and suggestions will be implemented with love for the glory of God through our Lord and Savior Jesus Christ.

REFERENCES

Brown, Carolyn C., *Developing Christian Education in the Smaller Church*, Abingdon , Nashville, TN: 1982.

Brown, E. Lynn, *The Pastor as an Enabling and Equipping Disciple*, Christian Methodist Episcopal Church, Memphis, TN: 1993.

Buttrick, George, *Preaching in Times Like These.*

Bultmann, Rudolph, *The Problem of Hermeneutics.*

Earl, Riggins R., Jr., *To You Who Teach in the Black Church*, National Baptist Publishing Board, Nashville, TN: 1974.

Everett II, David Leon, *In the Christian Teacher's Workshop*, National Baptist Publishing, Nashville, TN: 1986.

Friedeman, Matt, *The Master Plan of Teaching,* Victor Books, Wheaton, IL: 1990.

Gangel, Kenneth O., *24 Ways to Improve Your Teaching* Victor Books, Wheaton, IL: 1974.

Gilmore, Marshall, *Discipleship in Principle and in Practice*, Christian Methodist Episcopal Church Memphis, TN: 1993.

Leavitt, Guy P., Daniel, Eleanor, *Teach with Success* Standard Publishing, Cincinnati, Oh: 1979.

Leypoldt, Matha M., *Learning is Change*, Judson Press Valley Forge, PA: 1971.

Price, J. M., *Jesus the Teacher*, Convention Press Nashville, TN: 1946, Revised 1981,

Rusbuldt, Richard E., *Basic Teacher Skills*, Judson Press Valley Forge, PA: 1981.

Soulen, *Handbook of Biblical Criticism.*

The Book of Hymns, Board of Publications of The Methodist Church, Inc., Nashville, TN: 1964.

Willis, Wesley R., *Developing the Teacher in You*, Victor Books, Wheaton, IL: 1990.